PUR
POSE

Praise for "PURPOSE: Master Abundant Living"

This book is a challenge to live the life that God wants us to live with purpose instead of what the world is calling us to live. Everyone needs a purpose, and when we lose it we tend to drift like a ship without a rudder. With Jesus as our main focus, this life can be a proving ground for the life to come. We all need to read books like this.
—**Gary Saunders**
Volunteer Chaplain & Board of Directors, Southeastern Correctional Ministry

Purpose: Master Abundant Living is exactly the inspiration and truth people aspiring to get the most out of life need. Overflowing with transparency and how to apply the word of God in a world that fails to acknowledge the how to's of life God's way, Dr. Gregory and Pastor Eunice Woodard present their life's experiences and how God's purpose for your life will always prevail. Readers desiring to overcome obstacles, doubt, and at times, endless questions about their existence will for sure find the answers, hope, and comfort they seek by the end of this filling read!
—**Nicole Saunders, Author**

God has given the authors the vision to write this book so others who are lost can be equipped with the tools required to find their purpose! This book is a reflection of their excellency, discipleship, and their daily walk with God.
—**Mrs. Suzanne Blackwell**
Senior Associate
First Financial Security, LLC

Purpose: Master Abundant Living is a gem illuminating the authenticity of its authors. The Woodards meticulously extricate spiritual insight from a wealth of ministerial experiences. Here, the readers will realize the magnitude of God's purpose for them to become all that He has created them to be: abilities and giftings that match His plans for their lives. You will be inspired to identify your goals and propelled to attain your dreams. Combining anecdotal encounters with expert guidance, this book expresses immense compassion for helping others master their life. Use this power-packed opus to arise every morning pursuing your passion! Congratulations Dr. Gregory and Pastor Eunice Woodard for an outstanding and insightful master of abundant living!
—**Apostle John N. Gray**
Bethel Restoration Center, Williamsburg, VA

PURPOSE

MASTER ABUNDANT LIVING

Gregory and Eunice Woodard

Suffolk, Virginia

PURPOSE
Master Abundant Living

Copyright © 2020 by Gregory and Eunice Woodard
All rights reserved.

All rights reserved. This book is protected by the copyright laws of the United States of America. This book may not be copied or reprinted for commercial gain or profit. The use of quotations or occasional page copying for personal or group study is permitted and encouraged. Permission will be granted upon request.

Final Step Publishing, LLC

PO Box 1441
Suffolk, VA 23439

For Worldwide Distribution. Printed in U.S.A.

Soft cover ISBN: 978-1-7342371-9-1

Dedication

This book is lovingly dedicated to our parents for training us when we were young, so that as we grew older, we did not depart from it. We thank God for their faithful examples, support, corrections, prayers, encouragement, and their legacy. We honor their memory.

Graham and Ethel Woodard and Willie and Willie Mae Artis.

We would not be who we are if not for God, our parents, and our grandparents, Bishop Sylvester V. and Elder Betty Woodard; Joshua and Lula Best; Ollie and Bessie Eunice Jiles; and Willie and Claudie Artis. Their life lessons and legacy have inspired us to live our life on purpose. They did not sit back and wait for life to happen to them. They had a plan and took the necessary steps to create what they wanted against all odds. We move on, looking forward because of their legacy.

May God use the message of this book to inspire people to continue to grow and learn how to live life on purpose.

Contents

Foreword	11
Preface	17
Introduction	21
Chapter 1: In the Beginning	25
Chapter 2: Living Your Life	31
Chapter 3: Living Above It All	37
Chapter 4: Power of a Vision	45
Chapter 5: Living Together	53
Chapter 6: What A Difference A Day Makes	63
Chapter 7: Enjoy Life	71
Chapter 8: Reality Check	77
Chapter 9: The Conclusion of the Whole Matter of Life: Part One	85
Chapter 10: The Conclusion of the Whole Matter of Life: Part Two	93
Acknowledgments	96
Bibliography	98
About the Author	100

IN LOVING MEMORY

AUGUST 29, 1938

OCTOBER 31, 2019

DR. FLOYD M. BLACKWELL

○ ○ ○ ○ ○ ○ ○

His anointed preaching was spoken of as, "Kicking up dust on a muddy road."

Just like every person have parents; every person should have a Pastor. We thank God for Pastor Blackwell and his legacy. For over 37 years as our Pastor, he has helped us to live our life on Kingdom purpose.

Foreword

Serving as a tenured pastor for over four decades, I've been engaged in numerous conversations with individuals who struggled in life and wrestled with their life's purpose. The one question that always surfaces is, "What am I here for?" "Why was I born?" and "What am I supposed to be doing?"

There is no greater frustration in life than that of knowing you are supposed to do something but having no clue as to what that something is. Most, if not all of us, at one time or another have wrestled with finding our purpose.

Meeting and becoming acquainted with Bishop and Pastor Woodard over thirty years ago was every sense of the word refreshing. As a ministry couple, they seemed to have nailed the coffin on the purpose question. Like a warm fitted glove, they worked together hand and hand in a seamless fashion, building a ministry, supporting each other, and pouring their lives into the lives of those with whom they came in contact. I've watched this couple over the years as they remained steadfast, unmovable, and abounding in the Lord's work with a congregation birthed through their ministry. Their perseverance, content, and success is in my estimation evidence that they are living their God-given purpose. There are some who know their purpose but refuse to accept it and to execute it. That's certainly not the case with this ministry team. They are convinced of why they have been placed in the earth. They are excited and enthused with the work to which they have been assigned.

Those who know and embrace their God-given purpose in life are those who are best suited to help and to assist others in discovering and embracing their life's purpose. The Woodards do this well. Countless individuals have found their way and are on the right path because of the guiding light that the Woodard's lives, example, and work has provided.

We all need someone to emulate. We can all benefit from individuals who are willing to invest time, offer direction, and help us to probe deep down with in. I know that my life has been blessed by several individuals who invested their time with me and served as a sounding board from which I could bounce things off as I sought to understand and answer the " why am I here" for my own life.

Most noted is the late Deacon Clinton Grandy, a neighbor and deacon in my home church. In the community in which I grew up, it was common for older adults to greet children and ask them, "What do you want to be when you grow up?" Deacon Grandy was one of those older adults in my community who asked me that question on more than one occasion. Deep down within, I knew, but I was in need of affirmation. I needed someone who could affirm the hunch that I had within. I needed someone who believed in me and my abilities. I needed someone who would offer me direction, guidance, and most of all the opportunity for me to explore and get in touch with my God-given purpose.

I owe much of my success in life today to those individuals who were there for me, who help me to come to grips with my God-given purpose. Because I knew early on why God placed me in the earth, I was able to redeem the time, accomplish much early, and avoid many of life's pitfalls.

Needless to say, like Bishop Woodard, my parents played a major role in assisting me in my discovery. The manner in which I was reared, the lessons that I was taught at home, and the parental guidance I received were all a part of the process that God was working in my life to lead me to my God-given purpose.

While I am forever grateful for my parents and others who played a major role in shaping, guiding and helping me to be who I am, I'm also mindful that the discovery of one's purpose begins with God. An internet article accessed on April 23, 2020, entitled "Finding Purpose" by Rick Warren says, "The search for the purpose of life has puzzled people for thousands of years. That's because we typically begin at the wrong starting point – ourselves. We ask self-centered questions like: "What do I want to do with my life? What are my goals, my ambitions, and my dreams for my future?" Focusing on yourself will never reveal your life's purpose because the Bible says in Job 12:10, "It is God who directs the lives of His creatures; everyone's life is in His power..." Dr. Hugh Moorhead, a professor of philosophy at Northeastern Illinois University, once wrote to 250 of the best-known writers, philosophers, scientists, and intellectuals in the world asking them, "What is the meaning of life?" He then published their responses in a book. Some offered their best guesses, some admitted that they just made up a purpose for life, and others were honest enough to say they were clueless. In fact, a number of famous intellectuals asked Professor Moorhead to write back and tell them if he had discovered the purpose of life!

Fortunately, there is an alternative to speculation about the meaning and purpose of life. It's revelation. We can turn to what God has revealed about life in His Word. The easiest way to discover the purpose of an invention is to ask the creator of that invention. The same is true for discovering your life's purpose: ask God.

God has not left us in the dark to wonder and guess. He has clearly revealed His five purposes for our lives through the Bible. It's our owner's manual explaining why we are alive, how life works, what to avoid, and what to expect in the future. It explains what no self-help or philosophy book could know. The Bible says in 1 Corinthians 2:7, "God's wisdom... goes deep into the interior of His purposes... It's not the latest message, but more like the oldest – what God determined as the way to bring out His best in us...."

God is not just the starting point of your life; He is the source of it. To discover your purpose in life you must turn to God's Word, not the world's wisdom. You must build your life on eternal truths. Ephesians 1:11 says, "It's in Christ that we find out who we are and what we are living for. Long before we first heard of Christ and got our hopes up, He had His eye on us, had designs on us for glorious living, part of the overall purpose He is working out in everything and everyone."

In this book, Bishop and Pastor Woodard have captured the essence of how one may discover his or her

God-giving purpose by allowing their life's journey to be transparent. Reading and reflecting upon their journey, one is able to see woven throughout their lives how God has been active, present, and working through them.

This book is a must read as it gives a real-life model with practical examples that clearly show how we can come to grips with who we are and why God has placed each of us on this planet. Readers may expect to come away encouraged, inspired, but most of all, instructed on who to answer the age-old question of life, "Why am I here?"

I offer my gratitude to the Woodards for their willingness to once again pour their lives out as an offering unto God so that others may be blessed. It is my prayer that those who read their work will embrace and live out their God-given purpose to the fullest.

—Dr. Dwight Riddick Sr.
Senior Pastor
Gethsemane Baptist Church, Newport News, VA

Preface

This book was not really written, it evolved from our life experiences. It represents the unfolding of our own understanding of life. We are forever learning lessons to live by in this life. Don't waste any more time stumbling through life. Take time to identify your purpose and endeavor to let your purpose express itself every day in every way, every time. Living life on purpose is living life to the fullest. Your best life is straight ahead!

Every reader is a writer and can be an author. As we live life, we are communicating to others our story. Everyone has a story, a testimony. It is critically important for us to share our own story, sing our story, and live our story. We all have a past, present, and a future. Life is to be enjoyed, not endured. Live life with fun and laughter. Let's prepare today for our tomorrow and enjoy today.

Henry David Thoreau, essayist, poet, and philosopher said, "Go confidently in the direction of your dreams. Live the life you imagined." So, we have written this book for people like you and us. We want you to believe in yourself as much as God does. We are writing to encourage and challenge people who are seeking to live each day despite the issues of life. God wants us to succeed, but we must do it His way. As we live life, we can count on there being some setbacks and disappointments. Don't get discouraged, the comeback is better than the setback.

Life's challenges are necessary to help us grow as a person. Nothing can hold you back except yourself. Learn to adjust your living while keeping your focus clear on your destination.

It is impossible to thank everybody who has helped us put this book together. Some, however, have been especially helpful. Dr. Dwight S. Riddick Sr. was a vital part of this process. Thank you for your special friendship, inspiration, and encouragement in writing our first book.

Since October 1, 1983, we have had one pastor, Dr. Floyd M. Blackwell of Miracle Temple Baptist Church in Newport News, VA. On October 31, 2019, God called him home. We praise God for his kingdom example, legacy, wisdom, counsel, love, and most of all, we thank God for him believing in us. We thank God for Apostle John Gray Sr., pastor of Bethel Restoration Center in Williamsburg, VA for his prayers, support, and leadership.

We are indebted to Dr. Dwight Shawrod Riddick Jr., of Final Step Publishing, who has made helpful suggestions and guided us through this project.

We thank the members of Church of the Living Word in Hayes, Virginia. They have prayed for us, supported us, and loved us. We appreciate your commitment to help us achieve our kingdom purpose of "Building a victorious church that lives the Word through the Power of Jesus Christ." Your faithfulness in advancing the Kingdom of God has consistently moved us forward in ministry.

We have much to be thankful for and it is our prayer that God will empower you with Kingdom influence! As we say every Sunday morning, we love you!

To the Woodard, Best, Artis and Jiles family, friends, and associates, thank you for helping us to grow and mature. We thank our children, Guiseppe, Tia, Franchot, Tarnita, Angel, and Takiera for their love, understanding, and for helping us to live on purpose. We praise God for our grandchildren, Hunter, Zoe, Miriam, Myko, Memorie, Justice, J'Syiah, James, Solomon, Kira, Gregory, Maliyah, and Madison. We thank God for the blessing and joy of being their grandparents. Our desire is to empower you to live life on purpose.

May this book fortify the life and purpose of every person who reads this book! May God help us all to walk in the victory He has provided for us.

Introduction

Eunice and I are inseparable. We do everything together, including writing this book. She is my best friend and the love of my life.

We have written this book to encourage you to live the life that God has prepared for you; and to share what we have learned about life over more than sixty years of living and more than thirty-five years as Christians. The words and ideas that fill the pages to follow represent the activity and passion of our life. Together, we have matured through a process that has spanned over three decades. By God's grace, we have become seasoned enough to write a book about living life on purpose. God made you *on* purpose and *for* a purpose.

Too many of us are just surviving or existing, living day to day, just to get by. We want to inspire you to live life, enjoy life, and share life. Jesus said, "I am come that they might have life, and that they might have it more abundantly" (John 10:10). We are driven by problems, people, or purpose. Having a purpose is living for something that gives meaning to our life. Some may say it is God, success, wealth building, or charity. If we are living for something, our life has meaning and purpose.

We give all praise and glory to God for the vision of this book. We write not as if we know it all, but we write with the confidence that God knows all, and He knows the end of our story. We will have some challenging chapters in our life, but it is not the end of story. God is still speaking and writing the story of our life.

The opening chapter gives you a little background. We believe we must always base what we believe on God's Word. In other words, we must find a scripture to hang our hat on. The Bible is all about Jesus. He has come, and He is coming again!

Jesus has changed us inside out. A few of the chapters in this book explain these changes. God has helped us learn how to live the Christian life victoriously and serve Jesus Christ effectively.

Finally, we have written a few chapters to encourage you to be in fellowship with God every day. People need to witness the reality of what God has done in our lives to understand what He can do in theirs.

I made a commitment to Jesus Christ October 1, 1983, at the age of twenty-five. My mother, Ethel G. Woodard, shared God's love with me. I responded to Christ largely because of her life and testimony. I was addicted to drugs and alcohol. I was functional, yet my life was out of control. My behavior was destructive, and the problems were increasing. God freed me from sin, drugs, and alcohol.

At the age of twenty-five, I was a single mother not knowing exactly where to turn. I felt hopeless and afraid. I remembered my grandmother serving, rejoicing in the Lord, and watching her kneel by her bedside praying. I returned to church, searching for the answer with a different mindset, hearing and receiving the Word of God. I gave my life to Christ in 1982 and never looked back.

Over three decades later, we still believe God is in the business of transforming lives! "For everyone who has been born of God has overcome the world. And this is the victory that has overcome the world—our faith." (1 John 5:4 ESV) Once we have a relationship with God, He begins to reveal His purposes concerning our lives.

We learn by tribulation or revelation. God has life lessons to teach us, and sometimes we learn the hard way, but we learn. We can't teach what we don't know, nor can we speak what we don't show. In other words, we can't tell people how to get to a place you've never been. This book bears witness to our life lessons. *Witnessing* means telling others what we have seen and experienced in Jesus Christ.

We have learned to love Him more, pray more, trust Him more, and to wait on Him with more anticipation. God's timing and His ways are always right and best. God reveals Himself, His purpose, and His ways, and He invites us to join Him where He is already at work. As you read this book, we encourage you to settle the matter of life with God. Ask God to save you and He will. Romans 10:13 says, "Everyone who calls on the name of the Lord will be saved." We must change to become the person we need to be. Change is necessary in life. We believe God is calling Christians to be part of shaping the culture instead of being shaped by the culture. Once we know God's will, then we can adjust our life to Him and His purposes. In other words, our focus needs to be on God's purpose not our life issues.

Living at your best is of great value and nonnegotiable. Your latter days should be greater than your former days because of the life lessons that you have learned and applied daily to your living. As you read this book, we believe God to help you have an extraordinary impact on the earth.

1
In the Beginning

"For I know the thoughts that I think toward you, saith the LORD, thoughts of peace, and not of evil, to give you an expected end."
-Jeremiah 29.11

Do your best; be your best. Your faithfulness is your preparation for where God is taking you.
-Dr. Floyd M. Blackwell

People may see us in our present, but they don't know our beginning nor end. They see you now, but they didn't know you when. Everyone has a beginning to this journey called life. We are where we are supposed to be, and we thank God for being right where He appointed and purposed us to be in this season of our life. There is a place that you are purposed to be and the decisions you make are part of the process of getting there. Don't be late.

We were married December 30, 1984, at Second Baptist Church, Newport News, VA. Our pastor of thirty-six years, Dr. F.M. Blackwell, officiated. With just three months of courtship, we joined in holy matrimony with our theme song *Lord, Lift Us Up Where We Long* by Bebe and Cece Winans.

We live together, laugh together, love together, travel together, cry together, pray together, serve together in ministry, and share our life with others. When we look at our life and think things over, we know God

> **There is a place that you are purposed to be and the decisions you make are part of the process of getting there. Don't be late.**

has lifted us up where we belong. We bear witness that God is full of grace and mercy during all the challenges of life. God gave us life and kingdom purpose. Living life on purpose is to be driven by purpose. God has the master plan of life, so we do not have to figure out this thing called life. Genesis 2:7 says, "And the LORD God formed man of the dust of the ground, and breathed into his nostrils the breath of life; and man became a living soul." His desire and purpose are to have relationship and fellowship with us.

There is a saying: "Get a Life. Better yet: Get A Purpose." The greatest tragedy in life is living without purpose. *Purpose* is defined as the original intent for something. Simply put, purpose is the 'why' of a thing. God gave us life and God gave us purpose.

We should make plans, but God can sovereignly overrule them to accomplish His purpose.

Each of us must seriously consider God's purpose and plan for our life. We were born with purpose. We waste our time, money, and talent by doing what feels good and comfortable. Proverbs 19:21 says, "You can make many plans, but the Lord's purpose will prevail." This verse portrays the contrast between our finite wisdom and power and the infinite wisdom and power of God. We should make plans, but God can sovereignly overrule them to accomplish His purpose. Say what you may, but the counsel of the Lord shall stand. He knows what is best for us.

Having a sense of purpose—a reason to get out of bed in the morning and to keep going influences our ability to live a meaningful life. Not only does a sense of purpose fuel a sense of meaning in life, but it also brings with it more time in which to enjoy that meaning. Living a life that has meaning gives us motivation. Research conducted at the University of Rochester has shown that having a sense of purpose in life not only increases the quality of our lives but may also help us to live longer regardless of our age. Experiencing a purposeful life means living in the moment while connecting the past, the present, and the future.

We have many life lessons that helped us get to a place to commit our plans to the Lord. A life lesson is a lesson we learn in life. It's based on the idea of learning from our mistakes. We have made our share of mistakes. There are life lessons to learn from the bad decisions we make. Time and experience can be excellent teachers when we learn a lesson from our poor decisions. Experience comes from our way of living, understanding, and the adjustments we make.

The Bible is full of directions about practical living—principles that we can learn to apply to our life. God has the answer to the problems in life and He has the power to restore broken lives. Read the Bible. Instead of questioning God, question yourself. What God says is the way it is, no matter what you say. Our behavior doesn't have to be controlled by our thoughts and feelings. When our life is driven by purpose, we will live life on purpose and not by accident. As we live day to day, challenges may arise to try to rob us of our purpose. Choose to speak life purpose. The power of life and death is in the tongue.

We are free to live, so speak life. There is a lesson in our pain, storms, and issues. The old folks would say, if it don't kill you, it will make stronger. His grace is greater than our pain. When we are going through, we can live through it. Everything will be fine; don't fret, it's going to work out. Your life is now. Don't let what you see rob you of what you don't see. Live now and prepare for the future. At the end of the day, what matters most are the people in our lives.

We are life-long learners. We focus our time on personal, spiritual, and professional development. This deliberate choice to value continuous learning is what motivates us. As a lifelong learner, we have a passion for continuous improvement and cultivate a growth mindset. Life is filled with teachable moments no matter the time or situation. This learning may take place in a classroom, church service, at home, on the road, in nature, alone, with other people, or in nearly any other situation that may arise.

God has the answer to the problems in life and He has the power to restore broken lives.

Life is the expression of the purpose for being. In other words, it is the power within a seed, when planted in the garden, grows step by step to the fulfillment of its reason for being. Life is everything that happens: people say, 'That's life' or 'Life happens' which is all the events of living life on purpose. There is only one way to learn and that is through action; one way to live and that is to live. Trying to learn without doing is like trying to ride a bike by watching someone else ride. It's just not going to work. We are all fundamentally hands-on learners.

The question is what can we learn that will help us live our best life on purpose. It will not happen by accident. Life is about learning and learning is about living, therefore we apply the lessons to our life. Living a fulfilled life means to be in peace with God and yourself. Appreciate who you are, be content with what you have, and learn new things to add to your life.

In the next chapter, we will speak on living your life. We want to encourage everyone to stay in the classroom of life.

If we change our thoughts, we can change our behavior.

2
Live Your Life

"Thou wilt shew me the path of life: in thy presence is fulness of joy; at thy right hand there are pleasures for evermore."
— Psalm 16:11

"Change will not come if we wait for some other person or some other time. We are the ones we've been waiting for. We are the change that we seek."
— Barack Obama

Ofttimes we compare ourselves with others, or we try to be who we are not. We are who we are, and we shall become who we become. You are the only you God made; we are so special to God that He gave us our own fingerprints. If we don't like our life, then we can change it. Our problems are only a part of living, so don't let problems distract you from your destiny. Every day is a day of becoming who God says we can be. Let the Bible speak for itself. The Bible is the story of God's plan to redeem us through Jesus Christ. When we let the Scriptures speak into our lives, we will be transformed by the Word, day by day. Prayer helps us to intentionally apply the Word in our everyday life. As we develop a fuller picture of God's Word, we must compel others to follow Jesus.

We love living. Everyone will have problems in life but living on purpose is the best way to overcome them. What does not kill us will make us better at living life on purpose. In this life, we learn by revelation or tribulation. We can learn the easy way or the hard way, but we will learn. In this journey of life, we all go through cycles. There are seasons of life and each season has its purpose. Just like fall, winter, spring, and summer has its purpose. It has been said, failure is a divine directory to success. We can fail, but God never fails. Failure is impossible for God. When it's God's will, He strengthens our hands and provides what's needed to keep moving forward; therefore, failure can lead us to asking God for help. Keep going and advancing your purpose in life. Make a commitment to yourself to not be defined by your past. Living your vision will help you to forget your past and remind you that you are still alive, so live your life with purpose. God knows how to make us a success for His glory!

In 2009, General Motors was bailed out, banks were bailed out, and wall street was bailed out by the government (taxpayers), all with the idea that they are too big to fail. The federal government stepped in and helped them to recover. Well, we want to remind you that God is too big to let us fail. We are too valuable to God and His purpose. God will help us recover from bad decisions. We must focus on who we are becoming, not who we were, not who we've been, but who we are becoming. Sometimes we view ourselves on who we've been or used to be. We all have made mistakes. We all have sinned and fallen short of God's glory. The good news is that it's not the end of the story. Discouragement and failure are two steppingstones to success. We can overcome our past with Jesus. Think happy and be happy. Focus on God's plans for living and not your past.

> **The Bible is the story of God's plan to redeem us through Jesus Christ.**

Focus on your future and who you are becoming because of God's love, grace, and mercy. It's true that it is easier to quit, but it is not more rewarding.

It is a good time to reevaluate life. We want to influence you to live the life Jesus gave you and learn from the teachable moments. Talking negative about people hinders us from living our life with purpose. Folks may say they love you one day and talk about you the next day, but don't give up on people. Don't let the wrong done to you cause you to do wrong. Two wrongs don't make a right. Instead of taking responsibility, we waste time making excuses and complaining. Pray for people, love people, and forgive people because love covers a multitude of faults. Stop the drama and get a life. Don't let your feelings get in the way. Talk about your victories not your defeats. Life is a gift from God. Choose to live life and love life. Live and share life with others.

It's true that it is easier to quit, but it is not more rewarding.

We must do whatsoever is necessary for our growth. We all want to be better and do better. God has a plan for us to live life at the next level. When we do our part, things begin to work out the way God planned for them to. Romans 8:28 says, "We know that all things work together for good to them that love God, to them who are the called according to his purpose." Amid our problems and storms, God will work His purpose in our life.

It has been said, *only a fool keeps doing the same thing and expects different results*. A changed life is one that has changed directions. The way I use to go about doing things, I don't do anymore. Two of the most powerful words in advertising are *new* and *free*. To be worth anything, it must lead to a changed life and right living. To know to do good and don't do the good that you know, isn't right. The old folks used to say: "you see what you want to see, and you hear what you want to hear." We see what we expect to see and hear what we expect to hear. We can see the best of a person or situation or the worst. The cup can be half empty or half full. It depends on how you see it. Our hearts can be so hard sometimes that we will not change because we don't have an ear to hear or a mind to do. Build on where you are going not to where you are now. It will require some structural changes, but in the end, it will speak for itself. You may be closer now than you have ever been.

The way to overcome is to focus on God's purposes. In other words, our problems can't stop us from serving God. God will help us to overcome obstacles. God can't change our life without us. We can get more of what God has for our life if we give God more of our life. Progress is impossible without change. We must have a mind to serve God and not be distracted by the issues in our life. God's plans are greater than our imagination. You have a great life to live and you must live it. Resist every thought to think small and be persistent in living out your purpose. We have an innate desire for something outside our natural reach. In the beginning, we were created to manage all the abundance of creation. God has more for you. We must refuse to entertain our old pain in order to move forward in our life. It takes more energy to hold onto the past than it takes to live our life. Greater purpose will be manifested as our lifestyle come into divine order and alignment.

The Bible says in 1 Corinthians 2:9, "Eye hath not seen nor ear heard, neither have entered into the heart of man, the things which God hath prepared for them that love him." We can't imagine all that God has planned for us in this life. Knowing our destiny give us courage to endure hardship and life situations. God always has a plan for us and a destination where we can have a hope and a future. When God says He has a plan for our life, He is giving us a reason to exist. He's giving us a purpose for our life. God's plan is for us to live to live again through accepting Jesus as Lord and Savior. Living to live again is eternal life.

Measuring ourselves and others by God's standard helps us to live our own life and it keeps us positive. We ofttimes find it easy to find fault in others while excusing our own faults. Before we criticize someone, it's wise to check if we deserve the same criticism. Judge ourselves first and stop being critical in our attitude toward others. We can only live our own life; therefore, we should have a desire to change and improve not be busy trying to change and correct others. In other words, deal with our own faults and then help others. God will help us to change our negative to a positive. The sky is not the limit. We are our own limits. It's about breaking our personal limits and outgrowing ourselves to live our best lives. We can't set the pace by looking at the crowd. Look unto Jesus the author and finisher of our faith and giver of life. If we do better, we will live better!

Life's trials are not easy, but in God's will, each has a purpose.

3
Living Above It All

Tainted wealth has no lasting value, but right living can save your life.
—Proverbs 10:2

Change is the law of life. And those who look only to the past or present are certain to miss the future.
—John F. Kennedy

We were created by God to live above not beneath. It's a privilege to be alive—to breathe, to think, to enjoy, and to love. Things will happen, but we can live above our weaknesses through the power of Jesus. Oftentimes, we allow the challenges of life to hinder us from experiencing the life that God created us to live. We lose our focus and sense of direction. We must learn to stay focused when we encounter the cares of life. When we focus on God's Word, He will help us to step out of the situation and into the promise of His Word. The Bible says, "The footsteps of the righteous are ordered by the Lord, and He delights in his way" (Psalm 37:23). To live right is placing God above everything else we desire. We all must make changes in our life in order to live right.

God will ask us to do things we can't do. It's called a God-size assignment. In the natural, Peter stepped into the storm, but in the supernatural he stepped into the Word. The power of the Word enabled him to step into something that he feared. Matthew 14:22-32 is the only account that talks about Peter walking on the water. As Peter kept his eyes on Jesus and trusted in Him, he was able to do something no other man on earth did—walk on water. But, as soon as Peter took his eyes off Jesus, he began to sink. We are called to walk by faith and not sight. Faith comes by hearing and hearing by the Word. It's time for us to live above our situations. Jesus promises that even with faith the size of a mustard seed, we can move mountains. But if doubt crowds out our faith, we'll start to sink just like Peter did. We need to guard our hearts against doubting Jesus' power. By ourselves, we can't do "the impossible." However, if we have faith in Jesus, He will enable us to do what we never thought we could. Things that are impossible to do become possible with a little faith.

When we focus on God's Word, He will help us to step out of the situation and into the promise of His Word.

If we want to live above situations, we must get out of our boat of comfort. We can live above people talking about what we can't do by making a declaration of what God can do. In this life we will have tribulations, but don't take your eyes off Jesus. We can live above the problems and the winds of distraction! The good news is that we can call on God to help us live above our life issues and drama. It doesn't matter who you are or where you come from. The ability to triumph begins with you. Things will happen, but we can live above them all. And much of life is determined not by circumstances but by personal choice. It matters how you choose to live. And, so, we challenge you to begin to make a personal choice and decide that you are going to rejoice in the Lord no matter what.

Living a victorious life in Jesus is all about living above our weaknesses through the power of the Holy Spirit. Living life on purpose will give us teachable moments about the grace of God. In 2 Corinthians 12:9, the Apostle Paul says, "And he said unto me, my grace is sufficient for thee." *Grace* means the good-will of God towards us. His grace is enough to strengthen us and cheer up our spirits in all our afflictions.

Many times, we allow the cares of this world to take the fun out of living. We waste too much time worrying about things we can't change. We encourage you to live the life God has given you. God can help us live the good life. Live it up! It has been said that instead of acting like a sour lemon make some lemonade. Don't be troubled. Just believe that better days are straight ahead. Live life, share life, and enjoy life. We live to tell others about living life on purpose. You may ask the question: how can I live the Christian life? Repent and invite Jesus (the Son of God) into your heart to be your Savior and Lord. *Repent* means to turn from sin and to go the other way—God's way. If we are born again, the Kingdom of God comes in our heart through the Holy Spirit. God gives us a kingdom mindset and helps us live the abundant life.

In John 4:6 Jesus said, "I am the way and the truth and the life; no one comes to the Father but through Me." Many are seeking a way, a truth, and a life. People can see a difference between Christians and non-Christians. Jesus is the only way! Jesus reveals truth to us and gives life to us. Too often, we underestimate the power of godly example. We can make a difference by living the Word through the power of Jesus. We must submit to the Lordship of Jesus in our living. We must live the life, enjoy the life, and share the life of Jesus. Live the life that He died to give us. Live it up, live on purpose, and live above it all! Jesus is the Resurrection and the Life!

Life has two rules: 1) never quit and 2) always remember rule one. God has given you a power that all the forces of darkness can't stop it. Refuse to be overwhelmed. Rise up in confidence. Your life has its ups and downs and times of clarity and confusion. Yet, it holds a rich meaning, one that you unfold through living your purpose.

> **If we want to live above situations, we must get out of our boat of comfort.**

Our purpose motivates us to do and be our best. You could describe your life's purpose as the life that you were born to live. Life's circumstances can pull us into survival mode where we struggle to make it day after day. We want to encourage you to choose not to give up or give in; don't back up or turn around. Don't quit on yourself or others that believe in you. No matter what comes your way, don't give up on your next dimension of faith. Having disappointments and problems are a part of life. Don't magnify your emotions, just edify your attitude. The question is what can I learn from it that will make me better. Life's challenges are opportunities and lessons to learn. Learning is acquiring information or knowledge or experiences that will help us to be better, do better, and live better. When we are under pressure, what's in us will come out. Don't let the pressures of this life get the best of your purpose. Evaluate your actions to see what changes you need to make and make decisions to act upon your destiny and not your situations. Change will come as we stop reacting and be proactive! Stop focusing on problems and start looking for the goal line of life. We can't live in the past and expect to move forward. Three things we can do: overcome our past, live in the present, and prepare for the future. You must believe, better days are ahead.

Our Pastor, Dr. Floyd M. Blackwell, taught us that failure is a divine directory to success. Failure is only an event, not a person. Conflict is not bad or good; it just is, and it can be a good teacher. Don't let situations and other people define you. Failure is not final. Second chances are available with God. Every day is a good day to have a good day especially when stuff happens in our day. God made the day and He decreed it to be good. We may have done wrong, but life has not done us wrong. We have made mistakes, but life isn't a mistake. Life is a gift from God, and God is good all the time. Be of good courage, and don't quit. You matter, your life matters, so live on purpose. We are not an accident or a mistake. You have a wonderful life despite the problems. Our lives matter to God. Who we are, what we do, and what we become, matters to God. He is working His plan into life every day. Life has a way of teaching us lessons to live by.

Living a fulfilled life means to be in peace with God and yourself. It means appreciating who you are, being content with what you have, planning your life on purpose, and learning new things to add to your life. Above all else, experiencing a meaningful life means living in the moment, while connecting the past, the present, and the future. Doing so gives us a clearer idea of where we need to go considering where we have been. Living a life that has meaning is one of the most widely held goals in existence, something by which we motivate and measure ourselves. If there is one factor that influences our ability to live a meaningful life, it's having a sense of purpose: a reason to get out of bed in the morning and to keep on going. Not only does a sense of purpose fuel a sense of meaning in life, but it also brings with it more time in which to enjoy that meaning. Having a sense of purpose is an important component in a long and meaningfully lived life.

Living a meaningful life is closely related to genuineness, to being who we truly are. We were created in the image of God. Many people struggle to be themselves for fear of criticism or rejection; as a result, they find themselves living a life that is far from satisfying or meaningful. When we are not allowed, for whatever reason, to be who we truly are, we greatly diminish the meaning we can derive from the life we live. The simple fact is that sometimes it takes courage to live. And it can take even more courage to live a meaningful life. It can be all too easy to fall into the rut of habit, seldom reaching out, or trying fresh, new things. People who lead meaningful lives put themselves out there, they try new things, challenge the way they think, and seek out that which they want from life. A good way to look at *courage* is to view it as an attitude of being willing to try something a little different in order to develop and maximize the meaning we derive from life.

Living meaningful means that we need to accept the fact that there will be bumps, bruises, and perhaps even unhappiness along the way. Doing so gives us a clearer idea of where we need to go considering where we have been. Life itself is a process, and viewing things in their proper context, particularly our struggles, is associated with greater meaning and a sense of purpose. If there is meaning in life at all, then there are teachable moments in our struggles. Finding meaning and purpose in life is an ongoing journey, a process that takes time, patience, and faith. It is not something that occurs without effort. We can fulfill our goals, develop a deeper sense of purpose, and live the meaningful, more satisfying life we were meant to live.

Every adversity brings new experiences and new lessons.

4

Power of a Vision

*Where there is no vision, the people perish: but he that
keepeth the law, happy is he.
—Proverbs 29:18*

*We must set our thinking aright, get rid of our
old habit of limiting God in our lives, and
begin to live with expectancy.
—Dennis Bennett*

We can't sit back and wait for life to happen. We must have a plan and take the needed steps to create what we want. There are many people who have sight, but no vision, and there are many people who don't know where they're going. Do you know where you are going? Will you find yourself asking, "Why am I here? What is God's plan for my life and for my family? What is God's purpose for my life?" The Bible says, "Where there is no vision, the people perish: but he that keepeth the law, happy is he." Without a long-term plan—without a vision—we will wander aimlessly. Vision is something seen as an image in the mind as a result of thinking. Don't doubt what we can't see. As a man thinketh, so is he. People with vision has a consciousness of God. In other words, a vision gets us thinking of doing what others have not done. The word *vision* means the sense of sight, unusual or supernatural perception. In other words, the 'God given' ability to perceive the supernatural.

We can have a vision of being victorious despite the problems that we see, and you can purpose in your heart that you are going to get through no matter what. Stop justifying wrong attitudes, wrong behavior, and wrong words, and work your vision to do better. Stop being wishy washy; stop having that see/saw mindset and be like that tree planted by the waters of life, and say I shall not be moved. Whenever we do something, we will have some haters, just make sure you don't become a hater. When we encounter problems, we shift into a problem-solving mode. We consider the situation and seek a realistic strategy. The power of a vision is putting teamwork into action to accomplish life's purpose. Don't underestimate people

We can have a vision of being victorious despite the problems that we see, and you can purpose in your heart that you are going to get through no matter what.

nor yourself. We want to challenge and empower people with vision to live life on purpose. If we going to go where we've never been, then we have to see what we've never seen before. We want to help you to visualize what you could become. Then you must stir up another to visualize what they can become, and they help others to do the same. Living life is the empowerment of rising out of our slothfulness and strengthen our hands with purpose. In other words, let us do it with vigor and diligence. Let's rise with determination to do what we were born to do.

It is true that having an idea of where one is headed helps in getting there. Lack of vision, then, is a lack of God's revelatory word. With this we understand that without the Word of God, people are "loose"; that is, we go our own way. We live without restraint. Ultimately, living in such a way will lead to death because to ignore God's way is to ignore the way of life. So, what is the remedy to such toxic waywardness? God will help us to make sense of our past, bring peace for today, and create a vision for our tomorrow. Proverbs 29:18 tells us: "Blessed is the one who heeds wisdom's instruction." We are blessed when we keep God's directives. Life is not found in our ability to obey a list of do's and don'ts. Our obedience to God and our keeping of His Word flow from a relationship in which we are loved by God and we love Him in return (1 John 4:7–10). When we fail to read God's Word and live it out in our lives, we become people "without vision." When we ignore God's Word, we begin to live without restraint to our own peril. Conversely, when we heed God's Word, we are blessed. God has given us His Word, and He calls us to be faithful to it. In keeping God's Word, we will find life and joy in Him.

If we can think it, we can see it. To do what we haven't done before will take faith and work. Folk have told us it cannot be done because we have never done it before. We want to encourage you to trust God for great things. There are no limits. You must live beyond the limits that you and others have placed on you. We must press forward in the face of external opposition and internal differences. Yield not to distractions. Many folks will not rejoice with you in your well doing and it's okay. Opposition can drive us to our purpose not from it. When we are criticized for our commitment to our vision, we must refuse to be discouraged. When we are under pressure, we must plan today to ignore the negative and focus on your purpose. We must set our heart and minds on accomplishing our assignment. We will face opposition, but having a mind to work helps us to stay focused on our purpose.

It's important to have an attitude of embracing change. Change readiness is being ready to think new thoughts and shift our outlooks for greater. There is no growth without change. We must let go of our old ways in order to experience the new. When things happen that we don't understand, we must expect to come out better because of it. Don't complain because you won't be in that situation too long.

We must get to a place where we see more than what we see. We must look above our situation. To thrive in this life, we must keep our thought process above our problems. If we are going to live life on purpose, we must live 'above sea level.' The term 'above sea level' refers to the elevation of land as it relates to the sea level. The Grand Canyon is 7000 ft. above sea level, and Denver, Colorado is a mile above sea level. Above sea level is used in telecommunication to determine the coverage of area and aviation for flight level. We will use the term to elevate our vision and faith. ASL: 'above *see* level,' not *sea*. *Above* means further up; overhead; a higher place than. Such hope and expectations give us great courage to endure anything we might experience. Ofttimes, the problem is we can't see past our present situation. We can learn to be courageous in the midst of troubles by looking above see level for the purpose of seeing what lesson we can learn that will improve our life.

We should live by what we believe and not what we see or hear. Many may believe in a higher power or something greater than yourself. We believe it is the power of Jesus Christ and His Word. We walk by faith and not by sight, *on purpose*. Living above *see* level is the nature of faith. Hebrews 11:1 says, "Now faith is confidence in what we hope for and assurance about what we do not see." In other words, currently, at the present, at this moment, not tomorrow or yesterday, but now. Living above *see* level is exciting because you believe or expect to see more. Faith in action. It is the substance of things hoped for. It is a firm persuasion and expectation that God will do what He has promised. You must be thoroughly persuaded that God can keep that which you commit to Him. Faith reveals to the eye of the mind the reality of those things that cannot be seen.

We can learn to be courageous in the midst of troubles by looking above *see* level for the purpose of seeing what lesson we can learn that will improve our life.

The Bible says we all are given a measure of faith. Living above *see* level has been practiced from Genesis to Revelation. The believers before us were honored for their faith. We can do tremendous things in the strength of our faith. God made the world by His word: He said, let it be, and it was done. In other words, the world was made by His spoken WORD. This world still responds to His Word. Living above *see* level is speaking His word in a situation and expecting God to move. It is by faith that we understand the kingdom pattern and principles, not by the naked eye of reason. We cannot come to God unless we believe that He is who He has revealed himself to be in the scriptures. He is a rewarder of those that diligently seek Him. In other words, if we seek Him with all our heart we will be satisfied.

Reading the Bible elevates our faith above our sight. Reading the Word of God will improve our vision and our hearts. Romans 10:17 says, "Faith cometh by hearing and hearing by the Word of God." God uses scripture to open the eyes of those who do not know Him. When we believe what the Scriptures say about Him, we would know Him. Preaching the Gospel is the means of salvation. Faith in Jesus Christ is the result of hearing the Word. Faith will be produced if preaching is heard attentively.

Faith comes from hearing the message of Jesus Christ. The Gospel is the best news that's ever come from heaven to earth. The beginning of faith is hearing. God gives us faith to live above *see* level through the Word. It is not hearing enticing words but hearing the Word of God and hearing it as the Word of God will grow your faith. Jesus can open our eyes to see Him for who He is. In life, we will have distractions. We live in a culture that makes it easy to become distracted. The lack of focus is called A.D.D. - **A**ttention **D**eficit **D**isorder. It's a condition of being easily distracted. Distraction takes our attention away from what we are supposed to be doing. In other words, we see what we want to see instead of what we need to see. Doubt can distract us from believing His Word. Distraction prevents us from giving full attention to God. The cares of this life can blind us from seeing God, and life situations can distract our vision. Distractions come from external and internal sources.

Too many of us are being defeated in the trials of life when God has provided us with the means to live a victorious life through Jesus Christ. If we change our thinking, we will see things differently. Obstacles in our path need not be stumbling blocks; they can be stepping-stones. We don't have to succumb to habits of life that are not right when God will help us to get right. Get rid of the negative thinking and develop a positive and victorious attitude. The Bible is a message of hope, comfort, assurance, and victory. Some say, 'I'm trying to change' and keep doing the same old thing. Get rid of that 'I can't do anything right attitude'; get rid of that 'I'm trying mindset.' Get rid of the stuff in our lives that have no eternal value. God will help us to see His will for our life and He will empower us to fulfill it. Faith in Jesus is not our availability to Him, but rather our ability to believe His Word. You have purpose. Your purpose, just like your vision for life, is immeasurable.

There are no regrets in life. Just life lessons.

5
Living Together

Who is wise and understanding among you? Let them show it by their good life, by deeds done in the humility that comes from wisdom.
—*Proverbs 10:17*

Everything in life starts as a seed—a relationship, a marriage, a business, a church. And nothing happens until the seed is planted.
—*Rick Warren*

God instituted marriage that two people may share their lives together. God didn't create shacking up, living together, nor common law marriage (living together for a period of time as "being married," without ever getting a marriage license), only holy matrimony. The person you choose to marry will have a great influence in your life and in the decisions you make from the point of marriage onwards.

We have come to understand thoroughly the importance of God's blueprint for marriage and we are living it out in our daily lives. We hope that you will gain insight from our unique perspectives on how putting God's plan into action will change your life and marriage forever. God intends each of our marriages to be a way for us to be totally fulfilled, but we must live as an example of Christ's love for us. We should face life challenges together, make decisions together and always act as one, because this is part of living together.

Getting married is one of the most important decisions in life, one that will influence the level of happiness, growth, and success, like no other choice. We've been married over thirty-five years, and life is worth living. As we mentioned in a previous chapter, we got married December 30, 1984, and our theme song was *Lord, Lift Us Up*. God has lifted us up through our journey of life. One of our most heart-felt desires was to build a family where we can experience love and encouragement. God's Word, marriage conferences, and marriage counseling has helped us to learn principles that equipped us to build the type of family that we envisioned. We have come to understand the importance of God's blueprints for marriage and we enjoy living it out on purpose together. Our life and actions are communicated in this book.

God's Word, marriages conferences, and marriage counseling has helped us to learn principles that equipped us to build the type of family that we envisioned.

With over 35 years of marriage, over 40 years of salvation, 6 children, and 13 grandchildren, we have something to say about the journey of life. The journey of life is like a car traveling on the highways of life. First, when you are driving your car, stay in your lane. In life, we will have obstacles, detours, and distractions. If you don't like the way your car is running, fix it. You can fix your life.

When we see a one-way traffic sign, it means you can only travel one direction on that street. Jesus is like that one-way sign. Jesus is the only way to God. There is no other name whereby we can be saved. NO OTHER NAME LIKE THE NAME OF JESUS! Acts 4:12 says,

"Neither is there salvation in any other: for there is none other name under heaven given among men, whereby we must be saved." On October 1, 1983, I was born again. My life went from junk yard living to showroom living. Most people never come to Jesus to get their deepest needs met, so they never find what they so desperately seek in life or marriage.

We remembered our first experience of driving was looking over our parent's shoulders. Who shoulders are you looking over on your journey of life? For fifteen years, we were seated in our parents' vehicles as passengers and waited for our opportunity to mature and be responsible enough to take the steering wheel. We had to take driver education class, and we were tested in order to get our license. We could not get our license without first getting a learner's permit. We were given a driver's manual that had the knowledge of the highway system and safety regulations. We had to learn the laws of driving and defensive driving.

Challenges are what make life interesting and overcoming them is what makes life meaningful. No matter how bad the situation may get, never give up on being together and living together.

The Bible is like the driver's manual. God gave us life and we must learn the Bible to learn how to live. We had to learn the highway signs that has become a synopsis to life's journey: stop, yield, detour, speed limit, traffic light, no U turn, and so forth.

We were issued a learning permit which permitted us to learn to drive being accompanied by an experienced driver. Life situations are like a learning permit; it permits us to learn to live and grow. We must respect the law and follow the traffic signs knowing that this discipline minimizes our danger on the highway. The vehicle has a brake and gas pedal. They are designed to be used one or the other, not both at the same time. There is time that we must speed up and time that we must slow down and there are times that we must stop. We thank God for brakes. When we turned on the road of our emotions, stress, and disappointments, we chose to pump our brakes to get back on the right road of life. The life that God gave us to live according to His Word. Living together requires us to use our gas pedal of praise and to pump our brakes of repentance. Two people living together in marriage will have challenges. Challenges are what make life interesting and overcoming them is what makes life meaningful. No matter how bad the situation may get, never give up on being together and living together.

Every car owner is required to have car insurance and you should also have a life insurance policy. Jesus, as our Lord and Savior, gives us free eternal life insurance. We are covered with the blood of Jesus and we are in God's hands. You may have heard of the Allstate Insurance slogan: *You are in good hands with Allstate*. We are in good hands with Jesus.

Before we put the car in drive, we need to make two decisions: where are we going and how do we get there? Road maps and GPS are tools of help. Do you know where you are going in life? Do you know how to get there? God, the Bible, parents, pastors, and counselors are very needful. We all will enter crossroads in life. We left

Hampton, VA and thought we were going to Matthews, VA, but Matthews was our crossroad to Gloucester, VA.

    It's not about where you come from, but where you are going. Just as vehicles need regular maintenance and gas, our relationship needs regular maintenance and encouragement. Maintenance and gas are critical to the performance of the vehicle. Same for marriages, we must work at taking care of the relationship. Love is one of the important factors you need to take care of. Marriage is a huge investment of time, energy, and emotion. Protect and keep contributing to your investment. Marriages are fragile. They must be nurtured and protected if it is to last for a lifetime. Get a checkup and buckle up because you are going places. Be prepared for the unexpected because people and drivers can be unpredictable. People will get in your way to hold you up; just put your signal light on and go around them. Stay focused on your destination and don't be distracted by the cell phone and the scenery of life. If we fuel our life on the opinions of others, we are going to run out of gas. Let your thoughts of living on purpose lift you into creativity that is not hindered by opinion. We don't know what can happen tomorrow, so purpose to enjoy your life together today.

    In marriage, the little things are the big things or they can become the big thing. The things most likely to keep you from enjoying life are accidents, collisions, calamities, or mishaps. Don't get bitter, get better. People will cut in your lane of travel and may even cause an accident. This can be a teachable moment. It will make us to be a better defensive driver if we be more forgiving of others. What doesn't destroy us can make us better. Keep it moving—life is a journey. We live in a self-serving, live-for-the-moment, do-what-feels-good, society. It's easier to go back than it is to move forward. When we can't see any way forward, we may turn back to what was familiar. When the way forward is hard, we are tempted to turn back. We will have detours, delays, accidents, potholes, curves, and open highways. Seasons of disappointments and despair will come to all of us; that is a part of life. Don't stop moving towards something better.

Let your thoughts of living on purpose lift you into creativity that is not hindered by opinion.

The best way to prevent the unpreventable is finding the correct balance with our mind as well as our heart. Life happens. A critical part of living life on purpose is staying focused and staying in your lane. In our journey of life, we must purpose to pull into the rest area along the highways of life. Things happens. Living a life on purpose is to plan for the unexpected. Therefore, our automobiles are designed with horns and hazard lights. There will be times that we must beep our horn to get one another's attention. And there will be times that we must put on our hazard lights to be safe as we disagree without being disagreeable. It is wise to have AAA and additional coverage for the normal incidents that may happen. In this life we all need advice, directions, and help. We would not be where we are today if someone did not help us.

We can relate to frustration, stress, disappointment, and discouragement, but we don't shun from God. Sometimes our life is not falling apart but falling into place. Our best living is straight ahead. By God's grace we will emerge from the storms of life into the sunshine of life. No matter what two people may face, it is possible to get through it together if you both have confidence in the marriage and in one another. All that life brings our way can't outweigh our eternal life that Jesus has given us.

You know you better than anyone else. So, don't be fearful; be alive! Marriage is another significant life change. Choose right, and it may be the most positive decision you ever make. Circumstances are daily lessons to be considered and gleaned for new knowledge and wisdom. Knowledge and wisdom that is applied will bring us a brighter and better tomorrow. It is depressing to spend time thinking about the way things are now and not enough time thinking about how things can be better. There is a lot to learn and a lot to do every day. What today will be like is up to you.

Ofttimes, we are so busy trying to make a living that we don't make time to live. Our lives are consumed with the cares of this world and we must find a balance. Should we give time to our families or our work? Should we go to church or go to work on Sunday? Our problems are issues of timing and priority, not right and wrong. The real challenge in life is doing what we should be doing at the appropriate time. The Bible helps us to balance our life. Marriage duties, parental roles, church involvement —all take place under God's authority. Our lives are the only meaningful expression of what we believe and in Whom we believe. Our real wealth and worth, lies in our faith. Living together in peace with some necessary stress give our lives a deeper sense of meaning.

Life is more than money, success, and recognition, but having the things in life in the right prospective. We all have gifts and talents from God to be used for His purpose. We can value, admire, and appreciate others without comparing our life with another. There are many different people on the journey of life, and we must respect each other and stay in our lane of travel. We must learn to live together as a family, community, and as human beings. The problem is not with God's ways but our limited understanding of God and His ways.

Marriage is the process by which two people make their relationship official.

6
What a Difference a Day Makes

Jesus said to her, "I am the resurrection and the life. The one who believes in me will live, even though they die; and whoever lives by believing in me will never die. Do you believe this?"
—John 11:25-26

The quality, not the longevity, of one's life is what is important.
—Martin Luther King Jr.

The weather forecasters try their best to tell us the weather for the week. This forecast is an important part of us planning what to wear and when to go different places. No one wants to go to the beach or park with a forecast of thunderstorms. When we hear of a hurricane coming, we often prepare. When storms are heading our way the weather forecaster give us warnings and instructions to prepare. It is a part of life to experience storms. We have

Be consistent and determined to always be growing, learning, changing, and driven with purpose.

destiny in us, and we are unstoppable and unmovable. God will help us to weather the storms of life. Some folks are so negative, if you put them in a dark room, they will develop. The difficulties of life are opportunities for personal development. When we hear of sunny days ahead, we think about getting out with the purpose of enjoying the day.

We want to encourage you to weatherproof your purpose. Having purpose matters. Live your life on purpose, rain or shine. We all know about having fair weather friends or being fair weather Christians. They are with you when the weather is sunny and good, but when the weather is bad and stormy, you cannot count on them. People go to church when the weather is good but will not go in the rain. Be consistent and determined to always be growing, learning, changing, and driven with purpose. Make the choice to embrace this day. Do not let your today be stolen by yesterday's issues. A day can make a difference in your life. It's inspiring to see the amazing things that can happen in a day in which you participate.

We must keep the proper attitude when we are going through life because better days are coming. Never forget your purpose. We achieve that for which we aim. We can be busy, but the question is are we fulfilling our purpose. Every day is a new day that has the potential to make a difference in our life! Don't let anything interfere with your destiny! When we learn from our past, it can empower our present and propel us to greatness.

Some days are transitional days that connect our times and seasons. The beginning of a new chapter of life and the ending of another chapter are transitional periods. No matter what happens in our day, it is still a good day. Choose to live each day knowing a better day is coming. We must live life to the fullest while we can, so that at the end of the day, we will have joyful memories. Our trials and problems cannot stop our better days from coming, it only increases our desire for a better day. We will come across people in our life who will say all the right words, but in the end, it's our actions, not words, that matter. We must stop telling people what they should do and start doing what we should do. God will reveal to others His will through our example.

We all have life markers. Some things we must leave behind and other things we must never forget. December 30, 1984, we got married; and January 3, 1993, we became pastors of Church of the Living Word. We never thought of living our life without our parents. During that painful chapter in our life, we lived with a profound gratitude to God for all our parents imparted in our life. While we are living, we are writing our eulogy. Our parents left us a godly legacy. Legacy is a life-long project, and it's defined by what we impart into other people's lives. What matters most is how we live not how we died. People may forget how a person died, but they will remember how a person lived. Your legacy matters. Don't waste your time, don't waste your day, and don't waste your life. Stay woke and get rid of idleness. We encourage you to live your life in a way you want to be remembered.

This is the day that the Lord has made. Life is a gift from God that keeps giving. Stop running from stuff and start running to God. Living is giving and giving is living. When we yield our life to the control of the Holy Spirit, He will work His change in our life. You can make a difference today because Jesus can make a difference in your living. It's easier to fit in than it is to create the space and atmosphere for others to experience change. When we are living our life on purpose, we don't give our time and energy to insignificant issues. We can embrace and fulfill our purpose in life. Serving God makes a lasting difference in our daily living. Our home life matters because it is reflected in the community, in the marketplace, and in the church.

We have been under our parent's authority and influence all our lives. Authority is connected to experience. We learned and understood the blessing of honoring and respecting authority. It is critically important to listen and submit to people that have been there and done it. They know what they are talking about. Don't listen to people that have not done anything nor been anywhere. This leads to dysfunction with no accountability.

Living above situations and not beneath situations is the key to living through situations.

I remember in 1976, as an 82nd Airborne Paratrooper, I jumped out of an airplane and my parachute malfunctioned and did not open. I crashed hard to the ground and was injured. God spared my life, as I used the authority of the jumpmasters, in a death situation. I remember when I got phone privileges in Basic Training. I called my dad to thank him for his authority and all he taught me about submitting to authority.

Since we accepted Jesus as our Savior and Lord, we have been under spiritual authority. Many people struggle with authority, but our blessings are connected to spiritual authority. Being under authority prepares us to have and use authority to fulfill our purpose. It is not control, bondage, or dictatorship. We are talking about living life honoring and respecting spiritual authority. We are talking about being in Kingdom alignment and walking in divine order by being accountable to someone. You are free to change your mind and choose a different future despite your past. Failure is a divine directory to success.

This is your life, a gift from God. It's precious and valuable. Don't waste time with foolishness and negative energy. Live it and give synergy to others. Drama, stress, pressure, distress, worries, and depression are life killers. Life is better when we are laughing. Living above situations and not beneath situations is the key to living through situations. Jesus is the Way, the Truth, and the Life. He will make a way in every situation. It is a prepared way for you as you follow Jesus, the Way maker. We rely too much on the encouragement of people and not enough on the encouragement of God, that is in the Bible. Psalm 118:24 says, "This is the day the Lord has made; we will rejoice and be glad in it." No matter how bad things are, we can rejoice. Think about it: are you breathing? Are you walking? Can you speak? Can you see? We have reasons to rejoice this day. Life is for living not just existing. God woke us up this morning on purpose and with purpose. Let this day be purpose driven not situation driven. This day is of great value. Stop looking back to yesterday and move forward on purpose. Each day is a gift from God with new mercy and new opportunities. We have only this one day, and we must not be worried for God has a greater purpose for you today.

Today is everything. Don't waste it. Let yesterday go and live in this moment. A new day is filled with possibilities and opportunities. Today is the most important day of our life; it's all we have. Yesterday is gone and tomorrow is not promised. Living by faith is managing our life by being driven with purpose. Live life forward not backwards. If we don't like who we are now, we can change today, and we will be better tomorrow. Every day is a choice to do better. We must focus on the good things that God is doing in this day. We encourage you to make the best of each day by faith and stay positive no matter what is going on.

This is the day of blessings; don't let distractions cause you to miss the opportunity of a new day. A lot of us put things off until a later time. Procrastination isn't good for our personal development. We say, 'I'll do it later," and later never comes. Today is the day to do what we need to do! We have put things off long enough. Today is the day of decision. Today is good day to make the decision to change. The longer we wait, the harder it gets. All we have is today, the present time. We got to work while it's day. Some get stuck in "yesterday because it's easier to live in the past. Others postpone living until tomorrow. Today is the day to live out your faith. Today is the day to live life on purpose. This is your day. Today is a good day to find your purpose in life. This is the day to open our heart and invite Jesus in.

Our future is better and brighter than our past. Life is about growing, learning, and becoming what God purposed us to be. We only live once. Live one day at a time and today can make a difference in your life. When you have a sense of purpose and a vision of where you want to go in your life, then you can live a better day and a better life. There is a saying that God will handle all your problems today; God does not need our help, so have a good day.

Appreciate each day in your life and have a good day.

7
Enjoy Life

For the wages of sin is death, but the gift of God is eternal life in Christ Jesus our Lord.
—Romans 6:23

A man who won't die for something is not fit to live.
—Martin Luther King Jr.

It's no great secret that giving to others improves our own feelings of purpose and meaning. Giving can take many forms, of course: donating our time, our talents, or acts of kindness. Our time, energy, passion, and commitment is of great value. We can't sit back and wait for life to happen. Life is happening every day. You must have a plan to enjoy life and take the needed steps to create what you want.

Helping others seems to be correlated with increased life satisfaction. Lending a helping hand can provide a sense of purpose for all of us. Enjoying life and sharing life work for the benefit of others and it helps us to improve both physical and mental health. In fact, studies show that involvement in community service activities such as going to church services is linked to living longer. When we are living a meaningful life, we will have a meaningful impact on others. Finding our purpose will enhance life's meaning while maximizing our positive impact on the people with whom we come into contact. In other words, helping and doing good for others is an important component of any meaningfully lived life—it pays real dividends.

Enjoying life is closely related to genuineness, to being who we truly are. Many people struggle to be themselves for fear of criticism or rejection; as a result, they find themselves living a life that is far from satisfying or meaningful. When we decide not to be who we truly are, we greatly diminish the meaning we can gain from the life we live. Growth cannot happen beyond our personal responsibility. The more we learn to be fully accountable for our lives, the more fulfilling our lives will be. We must be willing to live in an authentic way, one that allows us to express who we truly are, even if this takes courage.

When we decide not to be who we truly are, we greatly diminish the meaning we can gain from the life we live.

The simple fact is that sometimes it takes courage to live. And it can take even more courage to live a meaningful life. It can be all too easy to fall into the rut of habit, seldom reaching out, and trying fresh, new things. People who lead meaningful lives put themselves out there, they try new things, challenge the way they think, and seek out that which they want from life. We must have an attitude of being willing to try something different in order to develop and maximize the meaning of life. Life itself is a process and viewing things in their proper context, particularly our struggles, is associated with greater meaning and a sense of purpose. Finding purpose in life is an ongoing journey, a process that takes time and patience. It is not something that occurs without effort.

While there is no secret formula that will help us find meaning, taking the right steps, on the right path will develop a sense of understanding of the process. Living your best life is an ongoing process. Be your best today and you will be the best of you. It's not 'how to do' but 'how to be.' We can become who God says we are by being who God says we are. Work on being and not doing. Instead of Nike's slogan, *Just Do It*, we encourage you to 'just be it.' Many of us do things that are not becoming of us. God will help us to be who He made us to be. Being is who you are and doing is what we do. Thinking through who we are helps us to think through our obstacles instead of reacting in our emotions. Think more for yourself and think beyond your excuses. We can't wait for others to do this for us. It is our responsibility. Think about it. Who told you that you couldn't become what God says you are? Often, we limit God by limited thinking. God can do anything but fail. It matters that we trust God. You matter and your thought process matters.

  We can become a product of our thought environment. How we respond to adversity and the affect it has on our character and our thinking is a matter over which we have some control. We remember growing up, we were asked the question, "What do you want to be when you grow up?" Not what you want to do but what do you want to be. What do you want to become as you grow? Inhale your future and exhale your past. Our tomorrow can be different if we push harder than yesterday. God is ready to assist us that we may enjoy life. We make excuses for doing what we shouldn't do and justify what we do. Life changes are a part of living. God will ask us to do something we have not done and something we think we cannot do. He wants us to trust Him to do it through us and for His glory. The truth is that we do what we want to do. The truth is that we can please God if we want to. If we want to do better, we can do better. It we want to enjoy life, we can enjoy life. We can do all things through Jesus, who strengthen us (Philippians 4:13). We encourage you to start living your best life today. Why wait until tomorrow when tomorrow is not promised to us?

      Challenges in our life can motivate us to seek God. You may be knocked off your feet and look defeated now, but you will stand again and live. Speak life and live life. Speaking life is telling people what they shall be and what they can become. We must learn to stay focused and pay attention. In this life we will have tribulation, but don't take your eyes off your purpose. If we change our view, we will see something new. Ofttimes, we allow the cares of this world to take the fun out of living. Life can be like a maze, trying to find our way. We waste too much time worrying about things we can't change, rather than investing the time to change the things we can. Just live the life God has given you and be encouraged. Eunice and I love to tell others about living life on purpose. In our day to day challenges, we must be the living proof that others may believe that Jesus saves. We must live life, enjoy life, and share life. Instead of acting like a sour lemon, make some lemonade and live it up. Don't be troubled, just live your life on purpose. Live up your purpose!

      We are created in God's image and our best life is in living in communion with God and other human beings. Keep your aspirations alive. To achieve anything requires faith and belief in yourself, vision, hard work, determination, and dedication. Remember, all things are possible for those who believe. Who is it that really knows the way for us to live our best life? In John 14:6, "Jesus saith unto him, I am the way, the truth, and the life: no man cometh unto the Father, but by me."

People know what we believe when they see what we do.

8
Reality Check

For God so loved the world that he gave his one and only Son, that whoever believes in him shall not perish but have eternal life.
–John 3:16

Believe that life is worth living and your belief will help create the fact.
–William James

Invest in what God says about you rather than what people say about you. It is easier to buy into the fake news (gossip, rumors, and lies) than it is to believe the truth in God's Word. Get some cheerleaders around you. Some people that know your purpose and believe in you. When you are down, they will cheer you up with a reality check. We have to get away from negativity and focus on the positive as we build our faith in God. Why settle for less when God has prepared better for us? Don't focus on where you began as much as where you want to end up. Have a vision. Proverbs 29:18 says, "Where there is no vision, the people perish: but he that keep the law, happy is he." Where do you want to go? Look forward to your destiny and not backwards at your past. We all have a brighter future that we have yet to live. We have life, you have a life, I have a life, and we challenge you to live your life.

Joint research conducted by psychologists from Stanford University, Florida State University, and the University of Minnesota shows that connection to others is necessary in order to bring meaning to our life. Being close to others, family or friends, results in a greater feeling of purpose and enhances life's meaning. When we are driven by purpose, we understand we must go through the process. When we are after the position, we take issue with the process. We want it now; we want what we see without going through the process or development. God gives us instructions for living in the Bible that we may live our best life every day. Just because a person doesn't believe in Jesus, he is still who the Bible says He is, and God loves him. He made a way for us to live our best life.

Life can be boring when we get stuck in one season **We have to get away from negativity and focus on the positive as we build our faith in God.** doing the same thing repeatedly. Fussing over the same problems and making the same excuses about life. There is a song titled *You've Got Me Going in Circles* by The Friends of Distinction in 1969 that says, "You've got me going in circles, around and round we go." We encourage you to get off that merry go round of life. It is TIME. We have been here before. Let's learn that lesson and move forward. At some point, we must wake up and see the big picture. When stuff happens that you can't control, get a reality check, get a grip on your emotions, and stay focused on living your life on purpose. If we are going to be in a storm, we would rather be in the storm with God, knowing after the storm, it will bring our next level in the place where God meant for us to be.

We can't be afraid of change. Stay the course. Change is good, and change is necessary. We must be the change we want to see in others. Holding onto something that is good for you now may be the very reason why you don't have anything better. What we do comes out of who we believe we are. The only way that we can live is if we grow. The only way that we can grow is if we change. The only way that we can change is if we learn. Living life on purpose is learning to redefine your purpose from season to season. The reality check is that humanity is seeking to find life and redefine life. Proverbs 21:21says, "He who goes after righteousness and mercy will get life, righteousness, and honor." Life lessons helps us to discover our purpose. Never stop moving forward; moving

Living life on purpose is learning to redefine your purpose from season to season.

to the next chapter is a part of living. If we are going to grow, we must learn to live at another level of maturity. Some of us stay where we are because of the situations. The reality is that it's time to walk in authority and get under authority. When we were children, we played games like *Simon Says* and *Mother May I*; little did we know that these games were teaching us authority and principles of life. Nursery rhymes like *Humpty Dumpty* and *I Think I Can*, were teaching moments. Submitting to authority is critically important. Submitting to God's will for your life is necessary. Your life has meaning, worth, and value.

It's a blessing to be under righteous authority. When you are submitted to righteous counsel, your purpose is established. We are submitted and accountable to authority. It began with our parents Graham and Ethel Woodard and Willie and Willie Mae Artis. When we were young, we obeyed their authority. As we became adults, we honored their authority and submitted to their counsel.

All our life we have been submitted to authority. Every person needs someone to speak truth into their lives. The truth that we don't want to hear but need to hear for our good. This truth is designed to help us live life on purpose.

We will have challenges in life but keep moving forward and we will experience a brighter and sweeter day. Somebody once said that the grass is greener on the other side. This is true. We will face difficulties but keep living out of your faith and don't live in the situation. When our life is centered in Christ everything else will work out. Adversity is God's most effective tool for the advancement of our spiritual lives. The circumstances and events that we see as setbacks are oftentimes the very things that launches us into spiritual growth. Once we begin to understand this, adversity becomes easier to bear. We must get to a level of maturity where we are strengthened by our hardships and challenges. When we are under pressure, our purpose is pressed out of us. Just like pressing toothpaste out of its tube.

It has been said that a mind is a terrible thing to waste. In order to live a life on purpose, we must examine the state of our mind. If we can manage what we meditate on, we will be victorious! Instead of thinking on bad things, we need to think on good things. The battle is in the mind! If we are not careful, evil thoughts will get in our heart and rob us of our purpose! Maintain the right state of the mind by focusing on your purpose. Philippians 4:8 says, "Finally, brethren, whatsoever things are true, honest, just, pure, lovely, whatsoever things are of good report; if there be any virtue, and if there be any praise, think on these things." When we go through our storms, let Philippians 4:8 work in our spirit.

Things happen in life that gives us opportunities to evaluate our faith. Don't give up in times of difficulty, just believe better is coming. Some settle for less when they can do better. Everybody has a past and everybody has a future. Your future is brighter than your past. We encourage you not to let the past rob you of a brighter future. Get rid of everything that hinders your purpose in life. Where you been has prepared you to where you are going. The good news is we can turn our backs on the past and look forward; things are getting better. It's exciting to start over—new challenges, new experiences, new opportunities. In life, we will face situations that causes us to wonder. Stay woke and stay vigilant. Don't sleep your life away. Don't sleep your purpose away. Wake up. Expect better, live better, expect more, and live more. Better and greater is coming.

We encourage you not to let the past rob you of a brighter future. Get rid of everything that hinders your purpose in life.

Eunice and I purposed to live to persuade others to believe that Jesus can save their soul. Do you remember when stores had layaway plans? It was a plan to put the items on hold by making a deposit and regular payments. When the balance was paid in full, you could pick up the items. Jesus gave His life that we should not live in our sins or our guilt. He purchased our salvation with the shedding of His blood on Calvary's cross and rose from the grave so that we can get right with God. Jesus offered the gift of salvation for free. No layaway plan or down payment is necessary. We can live right now for Jesus and live later with Jesus. We can have life more abundantly and our faith in Jesus will conquer our struggle with unbelief. Life will never make sense until we understand that we were made by God and for God's purposes.

People search all over the world for treasure; the real treasure is in you.

9

The Conclusion of the Whole Matter of Life: Part One

Greater love hath no man than this, that a man lay down his life for his friends.
—John 15:13

"The ultimate measure of a man is not where he stands in moments of comfort and convenience, but where he stands at times of challenge and controversy."
—Martin L. King Jr.

The date you were born and the date you died aren't what really matter. It's "the dash"— those years in between and what you do with them— that does. The things that matter most should make a difference in your life and in the lives of others. Life is fragile. James 4:14 says, "Life is like a vapor that appears for a brief moment and then vanishes away." When we go to the cemetery there is a name, two dates and a dash on the headstone. The little dash represents our life. Sometimes the line is so thin between life and death, but it summarizes our earthy existence.

We never know when our last day on earth will be, so, keep believing and hoping with all your might. It's better to have lived on purpose and discovered life than to have lived halfheartedly and died long before you ever stopped breathing. William Barclay once said, "There are two great days in a person's life – the day we are born and the day we discover why." Death is our constant companion, and it is death that reveals each person's life in the obituary. We do not remember days, we remember moments. The richness of our life lies in memories we leave for others to cherish. Our legacy matters. How we live in the present will reflect how we will be remembered. You are not what you feel nor what others may see. Your situation or failures do not define you. God knows who you are. Ofttimes people live and die never discovering who they are. There is greatness and purpose in you; tap

The date you were born and the date you died aren't what really matter. It's "the dash"— those years in between and what you do with them— that does.

into your potential and worth. You are of great value to the Lord. There is a message in our pain, storm, and issues.

If you're living, breathing, and doing anything of value, you will make mistakes. It's simply a fact of life. Don't let your past defeat you. The only kinds of people who don't make mistakes are dead people and people who are not doing anything. If you assume you don't make mistakes, you've just made one! Keep living and you will make mistakes. Life is worth living, and living with meaning and purpose matters. Rev. Martin Luther King Jr. said, "Our lives begin to end the day we become silent about things that matter." Live your best life now and continue to grow. The journey of life has its twist and turns, but God knows what the end will be. God knows our future. God knows our goings and comings. It's more to living than working on an eight-hour job. Living is experiencing life with God. Never give up on God because God will never give up on us.

Our sin, mistakes, and shortcomings are not bigger than God's forgiveness. When we are faced with who we are, God will help us to become who He says we are. Jesus says in John 19:30, "It is finished," He paid the debt of all sins in full on the cross. We can't let our guilt, shame, and past stop us from coming to God in repentance. When we repent of our sin, we turn from sin and turn to God. We forgive, God forgives, and we live life on purpose. God's mercy, forgiveness, and providence is real and powerful. It is never too late to turn to God and live life on purpose. Now is the best time. God will help us to look forward and move forward. Every word of Scripture is true. It contains answers to our questions and is applicable to the situations and problems we face in life. We need to allow the Bible to instruct us how to live our lives. This is done through consistent reading, study, and memorizing God's Word.

We have a purpose and calling. You have a purpose for being here! Who are you and why are you here? The key to knowing who you are is knowing who God is. The less of God you know, the more confused you become. If we look, we will find that there are clues to our purpose everywhere. Finding our purpose in life is critical. In God's eyes, we are treasured and valued. He knew us before we were in our mother's womb, and He has a purpose for our life, or we wouldn't be here. The first step in finding our purpose is understanding God can talk to us. God speaks through church services, through preachers, through circumstances, and through other people. And He always speaks through His Word. God has a plan for your life. He will speak to you. God has appointed you to be a life-changing person! He's going to put you in circumstances unique to you. As we take inventory of the many things we have experienced in our life, for good and bad, if we are open to the Lord, He will show us His plan for our future.

The conclusion of the whole matter is how will you define yourself. It's important to live a life that matters. Having a sense of purpose is an important component in a long and meaningful life. What will your legacy reflect? The things you do for yourself are gone when you are gone, but the things you do for others remain as your legacy. We only live once, so live right, live on purpose, and once is enough. This day is yours, a gift from God! Be responsible, seize this moment and allow it to propel you to the high levels of an empowered life. In this moment, plant the seeds of your legacy. Legacy is a life-long project, and it's defined by how you impart into other people's lives. Start today!

In our daily lives, we must see that we have been gifted another day to build our legacy on purpose. Participate in your legacy today. There are unlimited opportunities available with this new day. We were born and created for a purpose. You are not an accident or mistake. God loves you and you have great value. Psalm 39:4 says, "Teach me, O LORD, about the end of my life. Teach me about the number of days I have left so that I may know how temporary my life is." The reality of faith in Jesus is a matter of life and death. Dr. Miles Monroe said, "The Kingdom of God is all that matters and apart from the Kingdom of God, nothing matters." The Kingdom of God refers to the sovereign presence and authority of God impacting the earthly environment. Jesus is still the only answer to life's ultimate certainty–death. The question is, "Where will you spend eternity: heaven or hell?"

We need to plan now for our homegoing. Death is not the last word. For us that believe in Jesus, death is the prelude to eternal life with God. This confident hope inspires us to live life on purpose. Life's final common denominator is death. Have you thought about your life and how you want to be remembered? There is contrast in the matter of life and death in three areas: life's priorities, death's finalities and God's realities. Life's priorities ask the question what is life about. What do we really have? What matters in life? What we have or who we are. The amount of money we have is not as important as the way we use it.

The dash on the headstone speaks of what we do with Jesus and our sin issue. We will leave everything we owned behind. The only thing we take with us into eternity is guilt or grace. Death makes things we thought were so important in life disappear. God's realities say death is certain. The question is not if but when. There are only two destinations–heaven or hell. Grace is available and free. What matters in our life determines our eternal destination. Jesus died, rose from the dead, and many don't believe He is the Messiah. But God is the Source of life, and He directly placed life within man. The only question is where will we live?

Knowing Jesus as Lord and Savior is all that matters in life and death. In a changing world some things are still certain: heaven or hell, life or death. We must help people to decide to live for Jesus. Jesus matters in life and death. Where we spend eternity is determined by our response to the cross and the way we live. Wisdom gives us the knowledge and ability to make right choices at the right time. Make the most of time because time that is wasted can never be recovered. Many of us waste time because we are busy doing today what we should have done yesterday and are not prepared for tomorrow. Many people desire to live a life that counts. Make your life count. A life driven by eternity is a life that counts!

It's God's will for us to succeed. We were created to be successful. Oftentimes, success is perceived the way society defines it rather than the way God says. It is wise to spend time finding out what God is doing and join Him where He's working. The Bible gives us instructions on making our life count today and throughout eternity. We encourage you to believe you can make a difference. God's view will always bring out the best in us. Elevating our faith will energize our life, and increasing our faith will increase our living. We can get so busy making a living that we don't take time to live. Whatever you are going through, you have been chosen to get through it with the help of God. Walking by faith is not about what you see; it's about what you don't see. Life is full of choices and choices have consequences. Our choices in life determine our destiny. Choosing life is considering the entire spectrum of decisions we make every day. A decision is required; we must choose, and we must act. In other words, the decision to choose life is not just one decision on one topic. Choosing life is an expression of an entire understanding of everything we learn. Choosing life affects every aspect of our lives and the next generation. We encourage you to choose life, speak life, live life, and enjoy life. Living for God give us a sense of contentment and purpose. We don't have as many days as we had, and we don't have as much time to live in this world. We must live under the uncertainty of life and the near approach of death and eternity. When we have done all, we must wait upon God for the success.

Our life counts when we use it to His glory. Rick Warren, the author of *Purpose Driven Life* says, "Without God, life has no purpose and without purpose life has no meaning." God has purpose for our life. Purpose always produces passion to act. Action takes place in the present not the past or future. Our action points us to our future. Act on your future by deciding today. A purpose driven life prepares us for destiny.

May God smile upon you with favor. God will make our faces to shine and put gladness in our hearts, as we live life on purpose.

10

The Conclusion of the Whole Matter of Life: Part Two

We praise God for our life lessons and the teachable moments. We thank God for helping us to live the life He has prepared for us. We wrote this book for whosoever to read and not as a spiritual/religious book for the saved but to inspire everyone to live life on purpose. We encourage you to live life to the fullest with the help of God. Jesus is the Way and His way is the best way. Matthew 7:14 says, "But small is the gate and narrow the road that leads to life, and only a few find it." Challenges come and go; choose to continue to live according to the Bible, which is the opposite to living according to our flesh. We are a collection of our past experiences. If you are at a crossroads looking for that next season of life, the answer may be found somewhere in the pattern of your life experiences. Your life experiences matter. Whatever your destiny, keep moving toward it. Whether big or small, clear or vague, you are worth it. The world needs what you have to offer.

Our life is affected by our attitude more than anything else. Our level of living can be determined by the attitude which we approach life. Our attitude determines our altitude. Remember, what we won't learn by revelation, we will learn by tribulations. Our spiritual journey has unforgettable moments. Our challenges in life are teachable moments. Expect the unexpected. Expect means to look forward to or anticipate. Expect God to do the unexpected. Living life on purpose requires us to change our thinking and actions. We will manage our stress or our stress will manage us. You are too blessed to be stressed. We encourage you not to discount yourself because of your past. Do not slack off or turn back; keep moving forward. Don't let circumstances or failures deter you from your purpose!

Ecclesiastes 3:1 says, "For everything there is a season, and a time to every purpose under the heaven. For everything there is a fixed time, and a time for every business under the sun."

It is our prayer that you will be the living expression of God's kindness. Every box of puzzles has a picture on the box, a vision of what is in the box, and what the puzzles will look like when they are put together. One piece at a time fit into the vision. One day at a time fit into the vision of your life. Stay focused, it can happen. Stay the course. God can bring it into reality. You can see what you believe. It has been said that practice makes perfect, and the Christian faith is a practicing faith that directs our lifestyle. We are to practice what we believe that others may see that Jesus is alive. People are watching us and every day we get the opportunity to live the life that we purposed them to see. Apostle Paul said in Galatians 2:20, "It is no longer I who live, but it is Christ who lives in me." Living life on purpose is following the model of Jesus Christ. He gave His life that we may be restored to relationship with God. You are here for a purpose. There is no duplicate of you in the whole wide world. There never has been, there never will be. You were brought here now to fill a purpose. Take time to think that over and live life on purpose.

Let no one come to you without leaving you better off.

Acknowledgments

Jesus answered, "I am the way and the truth and the life. No one comes to the Father except through me.
—John 14:6

If you can't fly then run, if you can't run then walk, if you can't walk then crawl, but whatever you do you have to keep moving forward.
—Martin Luther King Jr.

We first acknowledge Jesus Christ as our Lord and Savior, and give God all the glory and honor for this book. I thank my wife and co-author, Eunice, for her prayers and continued confidence in God using us to write this book.

It takes a village to raise a child is an African proverb which means the responsibility of raising a child does not lie in the parents alone, but also with the extended family and in some cases the whole community. Thanks be to God for our family of aunts, uncles, siblings, neighbors, and a special shout out to our oldest sisters Arnita and Carolyn.

Thanks to all the men and women of God that has made a kingdom deposit in our lives over the years of our spiritual journey. Special thanks to Dr. Floyd M. Blackwell of Miracle Temple Baptist Church, Newport News, VA; Dr. L. W. Francisco III of Calvary Community Church, Hampton, VA.; Dr. B. Courtney McBath of

Calvary Revival Church, Norfolk, VA; Pastor Keith Parham of First Baptist Church, Hockley, Plainview, VA; and Bishop Dwight S. Riddick of, Gethsemane Baptist Church, Newport News, VA. Thank you for helping us to live life on purpose.

Trust in God's promises for your life and live life on purpose!

Bibliography

Blackaby, H.T. & King, C.V. (1994) Experiencing God. Nashville, TN: Broadman & Holman.

Blanchard, K. & Bowles, S. (1998) Gung Ho! New York, NY: Morrow.

Bryant, Alton T. (1967) The New Compact Bible Dictionary. Grand Rapids, MI: Zondervan Publishing House.

Dean, K.C. & Foster, R. (1998) The Godbearing Life. Nashville, TN: Upper Room.

Harris, J.H. (2002) The Courage To Lead. Landam, MD: Rowman & Littlefield.

Halliburton, W.J. (1986) Martin L. King Jr., I Have A Dream. New York, N.Y: Harper Collins.

Henry, Matthew, Commentary on the Whole Bible, Old Tappan, NJ; Fleming H. Revell Co.

Hybels, B. (2009) Courageous Leadership. Grand Rapids, Michigan: Zondervan.

Jenkins, Jerry. (1989) Loving Your Marriage Enough to Protect It. Chicago, IL: Moody Press.

McBath, B.C. (2008) Living @the Next Level. New York NY: Howard Books.

McCalep, G.O. (1997) Breaking the Huddle. Lithonia, GA: Orman.

Morley, Patrick (1990) Submitting to Christ in the Details of Life. Dallas, TX: Word Publishing.

Riddick, D.S. (2018) Reflections: Life Lessons I Learned from My Dad. Newport News, VA: Final Step Publishing.

Standfield, J.L. (2009) God, You Said... Bloomington, IN: Author House.

The New Thompson Chain Reference Bible (1964); Indianapolis, IN: B.B. Kirkbride Bible Co,

Tozer, A.W. (2014) The Pursuit Of God. New York, NY: Millennium.

Warren, R. (1995) The Purpose Driven Church. Grand Rapids, Michigan: Zondervan.

Wilson, M.C. (2009) Leaders in Motion. Arlington, VA: Transformation.

About the Authors

Pastor Eunice C. Woodard (born October 24, 1953) is the helpmeet of Dr. Gregory Woodard (born April 9, 1957), Bishop of Church of the Living Word in Gloucester, Virginia. They aspire to reach their community, city, and world with the gospel presented in a relevant and progressive way. They have been married since 1984.

Pastor Eunice was born and raised in Newport News, Virginia, and graduated from Bethel High School. After graduation, she attended Virginia Union University, majoring in Sociology. She attended Boyce Bible College (1998), a division of Southern Baptist Theological Seminary, with certificates of New Testament Studies. She holds a Bachelor of Theology (2020) from the Christian Bible College and Seminary.

Pastor Eunice Woodard was employed at the Newport News Shipbuilding and also Kinder-Care Learning Center, Inc. as a preschool teacher and promoted to Director. She surrendered to God and enter full-time ministry where she is an Executive Pastor, overseeing Administration, Sunday School, Women Ministry, Usher, and Praise Team as well as several other ministries.

In September 1983, Pastor Eunice Woodard accepted Jesus Christ as her Lord and Savior, under the pastorate of Rev. Floyd M. Blackwell, Second Baptist Church, Newport News, Virginia. On February 19, 1995, she was licensed to preach the Gospel by Bishop Gregory Woodard and ordained on March 1, 1998.

Dr. Gregory Woodard served three years in the U.S. Army, ending his career in the 82nd Airborne Unit, Ft. Bragg, N. C. He attended Thomas Nelson Community College with honors in Occupational Safety/Health. Dr. Woodard received a Bachelor of Theology (2000), Master of Divinity (2017), and a Doctor of Theology (2019) from Christian Bible College and Seminary.

While seeking a better way of life, (October 1, 1983) Dr. Woodard accepted Jesus Christ as his Lord and Savior and and joined Second Baptist Church. On May 28, 1989, he was licensed to preach the gospel by his pastor, Dr. Floyd M. Blackwell. He was ordained by the Peninsula Baptist Pastor's Council on January 27, 1991, at Miracle Temple (formerly Second Baptist Church), Newport News, Virginia. Dr. Gregory and Pastor Eunice Woodard are under the covering of Apostle John N. Gray, Sr., Bethel Restoration Center, Williamsburg, Virginia.

He has served on the Board of Directors of the Southeastern Correctional Ministry; President of the Gloucester Ministerial Association, member of the Minority Task Force of Gloucester, member of the Family Life Advisory Committee, the Gloucester Methamphetamine Task Force, the Board of Social Service, Gloucester

Planning Commission, the Board of Supervisors, Community Criminal Justice Board, Gloucester Community Policy Management Team, Hampton Roads Planning Commission, National Association of County Officials, Virginia Association of County of Officials and a Guest Teacher of Gloucester Public Schools..

Dr. Woodard is the founder of Church of the Living Word, birthed in January of 1993, and Vice President of Life Touch Fellowship. His well-rounded ministry is balanced in the knowledge of God's Word. God has anointed and equipped Dr. Gregory and Pastor Eunice Woodard as His ambassadors. God has given them a spirit like David's, a spirit which is designed to gracefully and purposefully watch over the congregation. They believe in submitting to Kingdom authority and encourage people to follow them as they follow Christ.

They are the parents of six children: Giuseppe, Tia, Franchot, Tarnita, Angel, and Takiera, and the grandparents of thirteen. They reside in Gloucester, Virginia.

www.ingramcontent.com/pod-product-compliance
Lightning Source LLC
Chambersburg PA
CBHW071019080526
44587CB00015B/2425